MW01073848

Why the End is Not Near

A Refutation of End–Times Hysteria

Duane Garner

Why the End is Not Near
A Refutation of End-Times Hysteria
by Duane Garner

Copyright © 2008, 2023 Duane Garner
Athanasius Press
715 Cypress Street
West Monroe, Louisiana, 71291
www.athanasiuspress.org

Cover design and typesetting: Rachel Rosales

ISBN: 978-1-957726-05-2

Printed in the United States of America.

Quick Reference

For Bailey

Introduction

In his popular novel *1984*, George Orwell provides a desperately bleak vision of the future. His story describes a time in which an invasive fascist government virtually eliminates all personal liberty and privacy and seems to be maniacally concerned with the tiniest details of everyone's personal life. We get the phrase "big brother is watching you" from this novel, because Orwell's futuristic government installs monitoring devices not only on city streets, but also in private residences, in order to be certain that the populace toes the line and that no one varies from government-imposed standards of society. When someone breaks rank there are severe, merciless penalties for misbehavior. Orwell paints an ultimately dehumanizing and horribly suppressive view of the days to come; the main character in the book sums up this perspective with the line, "If you want a vision of the future, picture a boot stomping on a human face, forever."

When you think about it, that represents not only Orwell's vision of the future, but also the story of history told from men's perspective. The greatest societies and most glorious civilizations men have created apart from God's law have ultimately resulted in boots stomping on faces. So, then, when almost all our contemporaries look to the future, they can expect no better.

Whereas at one time fictional depictions of the future in books and comics and television programs told all about the wonders of science and the heights of man's potential (like early *Star Trek*, perhaps), today's artistic forecasts of the future are dark, pessimistic affairs. Think of the recently popular *Matrix* movies, or *Terminator, Blade Runner, Planet of the Apes, A.I., Children of Men,* and *I Am Legend.* It seems that popular artistic expressions of the future all tell the story of a defeated, dehumanized, and desperate race of men. Men have destroyed their culture; society is in shambles. Only a few brave souls maintain their dignity, nobility, and heroism, while the rest of the race is killed or devolves into animals. If these accounts are more than fiction, if they accurately reflect the direction of the world, then we do not have much to look forward to.

Beyond movies, radical environmentalism tells us that we have only the scantest amount of time remaining before the world succumbs to our hairspray, hamburger wrappers, and carbon dioxide emissions. If we continue having kids, driving cars, and cutting down trees, we are just going to use the world up and one day we will all be wandering around in a post-apocalyptic wasteland.

Every few years we are told of a new crisis or a new danger that humans are subjecting the planet to. Not that long ago, we heard lots of scary warnings about ozone layer depletion. When I was a boy in the early eighties, my science textbooks warned of a coming global ice age, with polar bears wandering the streets of abandoned northern cities. That fear has been replaced by a new one. Today, of course, global warming is the threat. The earth, they tell us, will heat up to an unbearable level, melting the ice caps and flooding the coasts. It will be impossible to find a decent place to ski. Ask an environmentalist what is in store for the future of this planet and its inhabitants and you will not get an optimistic outlook.

The conventional wisdom of our day says that the human race is in decline, and things will only get worse. There is no longer much hope in the world for a future without war, without famine, without debt and disease. As Merle Haggard winsomely sang, "Is the best of the free life behind us now, and are the good times really over for good?"

Even with all of the popular pessimism, we would expect the Christian church to be the lighthouse of hope, to liberate the human imagination from the prospect of a continued downward spiral. Surely the church has maintained an optimistic outlook on the future—one that includes a vision for the restoration of the earth and peace among men. Sadly, that is not the case in much of North American evangelicalism.

Within the broadest branches of Christianity, over the last several decades, there has been the constant hammering of the message that the world will end at any minute. We have witnessed the innovation of an entire industry of Christian fiction that speaks of a future in which God's people are not victorious, but rather have diminished to such a small number that they are nearly hopeless and helpless. The church has chimed in with the worst science-fiction perspectives on the future together with the most extreme environmentalist Chicken Littles, and has offered a view of the future that is no better than Orwell's vision of a boot stomping on a human face, forever.

The radical environmentalist, the science fiction writer, and the evangelical have become strange partners on this issue, but the burning question remains: what vision of the future does the Bible present? The Scriptures teach us that if you want a vision of the future, picture a foot crushing the head of a serpent, forever. God promises us that we are not on the losing end of history. The story of the church is not ultimately one of defeat, of being overthrown or subjugated to Satan, the world, or any other tyranny. Rather, God has promised that in Christ we are triumphant over Satan and his minions.

This little book is my effort to demonstrate that the doctrines of hopelessness and pessimism are relatively new, they do not reflect the teaching of the Scriptures, and they are ultimately destructive for the church and her mission to disciple the nations. The church must have a markedly different message for the world than the one the world has drummed up for itself. It is a message of hope and salvation, reclamation and redemption—a message that sadly has been neglected for too long. Let's recover that message of hope together!

Understanding Dispensationalism

The year 2000 came and Jesus did not. For at least a generation, evangelicals and fundamentalists have strongly suggested that the years preceding the dawn of the twenty-first century might well be the last this old world would ever know. "There's not much time left," they have written, "We are so close to the final, climactic stages of world history."[1] It is of a certainty for them that "the time is short. Everything points to it. All

---

1. Hal Lindsey, *Planet Earth—2000 A.D.: Will Mankind Survive?* (Western Front Ltd., 1994), 3.

the evidence has piled up."[2] Of course, "every dedicated Bible student agrees that we must be near the point in time when Jesus will come again,"[3] for "planet earth is wearing out."[4] Without reservation or qualification, they preach the same message repeatedly and feverishly. That is, the second coming of Jesus is sure to happen in our day, and woe upon anyone who is not ready for the grand event.

Yet we are now well into the twenty-first century, and as the majority of evangelicals and fundamentalists grow the gray hair they never thought they would grow, and see the grandchildren they never thought they would see, they must either rethink their concept of the end of the world, or consider the possibility that they have all been left behind. Theirs is an eschatology that depends more heavily on the evidences they see in the world around them than on the Scriptures and the historical doctrines of the church. Since the key bit of experiential evidence for their position (the

---

2. Edgar C. Whisenant, "88 Reasons Why the Rapture Will Be in 1988" and "The Final Shout: Rapture Report: 1989," quoted by Gary North in *Rapture Fever* (Tyler, TX: Institute for Christian Economics, 1993), 25.

3. L. D. Foreman, *The Bible in Eight Ages* (Texarkana, TX: Bogard Press, 1955), 411.

4. Ibid., 416.

"rapture" of the church) has not been produced, one is left to wonder how much longer people will continue to adopt an eschatological system that for more than a century and a half has proclaimed, with no substantial development to back the claims, that the end of the world could come at any moment.

This particular view of the future is not the product of serious biblical scholarship, but rather the product of a sensationalistic element in the church. It dates back not earlier than the beginning of the nineteenth century, and is entirely contrary to the biblical concept of the "end times." Wherever this doctrine has been applied, it has done immeasurable harm to the church and distracted her from her mission.

Countless good, sincere Christian people have been drawn into adopting a system of reading the Bible that leads them to the conclusion that the "any-minute-now" return of Christ is the only acceptable, orthodox understanding of how the Scriptures speak about the second coming of Christ and the future of the world. The great majority of evangelicals and fundamentalists have never been taught—and few have even heard of—any other method of interpreting the prophetic passages in the Bible. Most would probably be surprised to learn that they are reading the Bible and speaking about prophecy using the framework of a theological system that was fabricated relatively recently in church history.

What is most stunning about folks who espouse this set of beliefs is that quite a lot of them do not realize that they are following a particular theological system at all. They become so saturated with this particular way of understanding the Scriptures that they simply understand themselves to be reading the Bible in the most plain and literal manner possible. However, there is a rather easily-defined set of doctrines that are fundamental to these end-times beliefs, and these doctrines are part of an innovative new theological system known as "dispensationalism."

The doctrines of the imminent second coming of Jesus Christ together with the rapture of the saints, the future seven-year tribulation, the future appearance of an apostate world leader known as the Antichrist, and the one-thousand-year reign of Christ on a physical throne in Jerusalem are the central eschatological elements of the theological system known as dispensationalism.[5] These doctrines taken together are utterly

---

5. It should be noted that while dispensationalism maintains that soon after Christ's return to earth he will establish a one-thousand-year kingdom (the view known as pre-millennialism), this view is not unique to dispensationalists. There have been many notable figures in the history of the church who have held this position, categorized as "historic pre-millennialism." While the historical

unique to dispensationalism; they cannot be found in similar form in any other eschatology.

To define the position more broadly, dispensationalism is a way of reading the Bible that divides the story of God and his people into any number of "dispensations" or "ages." In these various dispensations, God establishes his particular wishes for a particular group of people and attempts to accomplish a particular mission. According to one of the movement's leading advocates, a dispensation is "a period of time during which man is tested in respect to obedience to some specific revelation of the will of God."[6] Regardless of whether or not man passes the test, God soon thereafter introduces a new "dispensation" in a new age with a new group of people.

Dispensationalism teaches that from the age of Adam to the age of Noah and from the age of Abraham to the ages of Moses and David, God continually presents new plans by which man may please him, scrapping all previous plans in the process. In each age

---

pre-millennial position has its problems, it is not under scrutiny in this paper. It is *dispensational* pre-millennialism that has had the worst influence on the church and has caused the most harm, most notably in its several elements which are unique to dispensational pre-millennialism and are utterly absent in other views of eschatology.

6. C. I. Scofield, *Scofield Study Bible*, note five on Genesis 1:28.

God sets up new rules and covenants—which man fails to keep—until finally God sends Jesus to establish another plan with the cross and the establishment of the church. This current church age, according to dispensationalism, was unknown to the Old Testament prophets and is essentially a "Plan B." God formulated this Plan B in response to the failure of the Jewish people to obey the demands of the previous covenants and to recognize the Messiah. The church age is not permanent, however, for God has yet another plan in the works.

Dispensationalism teaches that at the end of the church age Jesus will return to take his people up to heaven (this is the event known as "the rapture") for a period of time while he pours out terrible judgment on the earth below, culminating in his victory and the establishment of an earthly political kingdom wherein he reigns from Jerusalem for one thousand years. This represents the fulfillment of God's promise to David of a perfect kingdom in which Messiah would rule. During this one-thousand-year reign, dispensationalism teaches that Satan will be bound, the temple will be rebuilt, and the sacrificial system will be reinstituted. Even *that* dispensation is not permanent, for there is yet another dispensation on the way. The millennial kingdom will come under attack by wicked people remaining on the earth, lead by Satan whom Christ has loosed. Christ will vanquish them and destroy the planet and usher in what is expected to be the final dispensation, the "heaven age."

It bears repeating that all of these doctrines taken together make up the system known as dispensationalism and are not put together this way in any other theological formulation, but rather are uniquely dispensationalist. This is a system defined largely by its view of the end of the world and can hardly be described apart from it.

It should not be overlooked that this view teaches in essence not *one* second coming of Christ, but *two* second comings of Christ. This is one of the most hotly debated aspects of dispensational pre-millennialism. All sorts of speculation have arisen around precisely how Christ's one return can be split into two separate events. Some maintain that the first coming at the rapture will be a "secret" coming, seen only by the church. Others believe that the rapture will occur closer to the beginning of the establishment of the millennial kingdom. There has been no definitive dispensational statement regarding precisely how this can be worked out, but the majority of popular evangelical dispensationalists today seem to maintain that the rapture will be a "secret" coming. It should also be noted at this point that the double nature of the second coming is one of the primary points of departure of dispensational pre-millennialism from historical pre-millennialism.

In dispensationalism, Christ comes first to rapture his church and then comes again *with* his church to establish his millennial kingdom. This requires a great deal of referencing and cross-referencing Scripture on the part of the dispensational apologist, for he must always be clear in his definition to *which* second coming he is referring.

Note also that dispensationalism reflects a depressingly pessimistic view of the success of the church and the gospel. It teaches that everything continues to get worse and worse until one day Jesus comes back (not a moment too soon) to rescue his people before they are overcome by the enemy. The church does not get the chance to complete her mission and the gospel falls largely on deaf ears throughout history. Dispensationalists expect ultimately that there will be more apostates than faithful, persevering Christians and they view a dwindling number of saints and a weakened church as good signs that the rapture will take place soon.

This highly-nuanced and arcane doctrine is almost never presented without the aid of a number of charts and diagrams. Such are needed to keep it all straight and even within the camp there is much heated disagreement about the placement of specific events within the timeline. For the dispensationalist there is no other way to read the Bible than to divide it into various sections, and to place the future thousand-year reign of Christ at the apex of the story of all creation. Without exception, the dispensationalist reads the words "end times" and the "end of the age" in the Scriptures to mean the end of the earth, and expects such events to be soon on the horizon. The imminent rapture of the church is a much-anticipated event, and for many it is the chief impetus for any thought or action.

The dispensationalist often finds it difficult to think outside of the belief that one day—very likely in his own lifetime—Jesus will appear in the clear blue sky and take him up to heaven. This teaching has had profound impact upon the church, most notably in the last twenty-five years or so, as some have found there is a great deal of money to be made in books, cassettes, CDs, and videos based on the dispensational view of eschatology. They have gained their notoriety and earned their money by playing upon the expectations of an untold number of Christians who would not be at all surprised if the world were to end sometime in the next ten minutes. The popularity of the doctrine has permeated popular Christian thought so completely that an entire generation of evangelicals and fundamentalists is not even aware of any other way of reading the Bible, and is entirely unfamiliar with any opposing view of eschatology.

The Origin of Dispensationalism

Many commonly assume that such a complex doctrine must certainly have been around for the entire history of the church, but by all indications, dispensationalism was developed in Scotland in the early nineteenth century.[7] Some historians trace it to the visions of a young Scottish woman named Margaret McDonald, a member of the Plymouth Brethren Church whose trances revealed to her that the return of Christ would be in two distinct stages. She dreamed that the believer would be caught up to the Lord in the air preceding the days of the antichrist and before a final revelation of Christ at the end of the age.

Others trace the view directly to Ms. McDonald's pastor, J. N. Darby, who left the Church of England to join the Scottish Plymouth Brethren in 1827. Darby first made use of the two-stage return of Christ in his sermons in 1830 and continued to develop the idea

---

7. *Holman Bible Dictionary* (Grand Rapids, MI: Zondervan, 1991), 370; *Dictionary of Cults, Sects, Religions and the Occult* (Grand Rapids, MI: Zondervan, 1993), 90; Iain H. Murray, *The Puritan Hope: Revival and the Interpretation of Prophecy* (Carlisle, PA: Banner of Truth, 1998), 197–206.

throughout his ministry. By his death in 1882, he had written over forty volumes on various topics concerning prophecy and Biblical interpretation. Darby can rightly be considered the father of dispensationalism, for he was the first in the history of Christianity to write and preach using the dispensational hermeneutic.

Darby made several visits to the United States and in the process made many converts to his new theology, one of whom was C. I. Scofield, who published the Scofield Study Bible in 1909. This study Bible was essentially a King James Bible with a running dispensational commentary along with the text of the Scriptures. By 1959, the Scofield Bible had sold three million copies[8] and is still the Bible of choice for many fundamentalists. Another of Darby's converts was D. L. Moody who, in his day, became one of the most popular evangelists in the English-speaking world.

Darby's theology swept through the church on both sides of the Atlantic and was in the process of becoming entirely mainstreamed by the beginning of the twentieth century.[9] Seminaries began to teach dis-

---

8. Murray, *The Puritan Hope*, 198.

9. In 1956, fundamentalist dispensationalist Baptist author and former president of the American Baptist Association Albert Garner admitted in *Bible Analysis* (Texarkana, TX: Bogard Press, 1956) that then-popular views concerning the rapture and the resurrection of the dead were not more than fifty years

pensationalism formally as a proper way of reading and understanding the Scriptures. It appeared to most to be an entirely legitimate development in the growth of Biblical understanding.

What is so curious about its early acceptance and growth is how it has always been perceived as a Bible-centered system, rejecting all forms of "man-made" theology, yet dispensationalism is itself wholly synthetic. It has no root in the eighteen hundred years of Christian thought that came before it. Its central teachings were unheard of before the nineteenth century and its origin could quite possibly be traced to a Scottish girl's bad dreams. It is quite clearly a product of something other than serious, orthodox, biblical scholarship, yet its most ardent supporters maintain that it is the only hermeneutic untainted by the dangerous "doctrines of men."

How does such a blatantly synthetic, extra-Biblical theological novelty become the predominant method

---

old. He writes, "A few years ago it was considered heresy to preach that there were two resurrections, one for the righteous and another for the unrighteous. But today it is generally admitted by most Bible scholars that there shall be two resurrections ..." He then goes on to detail his theory that only those who are members of Baptist churches and who are looking for the coming of Christ will be raptured and proceeds to defend himself against charges of heresy by writing "[t]his position is considered by some to be just as heretical as the idea of a different time element for the resurrection of the just and the unjust was some fifty years ago."

of Biblical interpretation? The answer lies in the manner it which it has been marketed. From its inception, dispensationalist writers have attempted to distract attention from dispensationalism's own spurious origin by undermining all other concepts, labeling them "man-made." All the while, they promote their own ideas as being the product of serious reflection upon the Scriptures alone, apart from any other influence. Christian historian Iain Murray writes:

> There can be no doubt that one reason for the influence of Darby's writings was their constant appeal to Scripture, and his claim, so repeatedly made that "express revelation" alone weighed with him. Thus at the outset of his *Brief Remarks on the Work of Rev. David Brown, entitled, "Christ's Second Coming, Is It Pre-Millennial?"* Darby tells us, "I have not thought it necessary to follow Dr. B. in all his comments on men's views. It sufficed to take up those of scripture." Brown, we are told, "borrowed enormously" from other sources; "his reasoning is the effect of judging new truths by old traditions"; confusion on prophecy is due to the fact that men "mix up traditional theology with the word of God." Darby, on the other hand, considered it enough to connect his interpretation with particular texts of Scripture plus comments such

as, "the smallest attention to the passage makes this clear," or "Nothing can be simpler or clearer." Again, "There are those who must have scripture testimony for what they believe." Someone who had never read David Brown might be pardoned in supposing that if this was the state of the case, the controversy for or against pre-millennialism was just a question of being for or against scripture.[10]

The final sentence caps it all. Dispensationalism has marketed itself in such a way that its students come to believe that to be against dispensationalism is to be against the Scriptures and that anyone who takes exception to their system must naturally have a very low regard for the Scriptures.[11] They attempt to gain a theological monopoly by stating, "Do not accept any man-made theology . . . (except ours). Do not read anybody

---

10. Murray, *The Puritan Hope*, 198–99.

11. You see, not only do they view the Scriptures to be inerrant and infallible, but they view their *own interpretation* of them to be inerrant and infallible. They easily assume that you will agree that their interpretation is the self-evident teaching of the Scriptures. To question their particular interpretation is not to question their teaching, but to question the Bible itself. This is usually the mind-set a dispensationalist will bring to any discussion. Therefore I wish to affirm my love for the Scriptures and my firm belief in their inerrancy and infallibility, even as I question the tenets of dispensationalism. Be sure that I am not attacking the Bible, but rather I am only questioning a particular interpretation of it.

else's commentary on the Bible . . . (well, you can read ours)." While dispensationalist writers claim to put the reader in direct contact with the Scriptures, and remove all distractions and outside influences, they end up cornering the Bible student into studying dispensationalism alone and prejudiciously denouncing all other approaches as the lowly products of misguided imaginations. This campaign has been so successful in fusing the dispensationalist framework together with the Scriptures themselves that many fundamentalist dispensationalists do not think of themselves as dispensationalists. They sincerely believe that they have gotten all of their theology from the Bible alone and have not drawn anything from any outside source.

This marketing program did not end with Darby. Modern-day Scofieldite and noted dispensationalist Charles Ryrie first published the Ryrie Study Bible in 1986. In one of the several comment sections of the study Bible, after critiquing other eschatological views, he notes that dispensationalism's eschatology "follows the plain, normal, literal, historical and grammatical method of interpretation."[12] Even though I shall *shortly* demonstrate how this statement is not entirely consistent with key points of dispensational eschatology, to

---

12. *Ryrie Study Bible* (Chicago, IL: Moody Bible Institute, 1995), 2076.

read it at its face value, Ryrie seems to be implying that every other method of interpretation is based on flights of fancy, indigestion, novelty, or Biblical illiteracy.

Remember, *his* is the system which grew out of the highly irregular Brethren movement in the eighteen hundreds. It is *his* system which has an origin possibly traceable to a Scotswoman's night visions. *His* is the system that is not supported by a single trace of writing before 1830. Yet he claims that *his* is the system that is *the* "historical . . . method of interpretation."

Perhaps Ryrie is suggesting to us that before Darby and Scofield, the church was in a fog without a good tool for understanding the Scriptures. If indeed this is his point, then it follows that we may understand him to be saying that all of the saints who lived before 1830 did not employ a plain, normal, literal, historical, and grammatical method of interpretation.

Summary

The view of the "any-minute-now" rapture of the saints together with the belief that some time after that event Christ will return again to usher in a thousand-year political kingdom, thereby fulfilling his promises to David, is the product of a method of interpretation known as dispensationalism. This construction is entirely unique to dispensationalism. No other system teaches this view.

Dispensationalism is fewer than two hundred years old. It was fabricated by Darby and further formulated by Scofield. Dispensationalism is not a development of orthodox, historical Christian theology, but is the product of over-stimulated imaginations together with a lack of honest Biblical scholarship.

Why Dispensationalism is Bad for the Church

As this curious theological system has grown in popularity, its secondary implications and practicalities have had time to run their course and work themselves out as people work and plan and live with its principles in their heads. If this set of doctrines does in fact own the purely Biblical basis that it claims, then it seems that we should be able to observe a great deal of good fruit as a result of its assimilation into mainstream Christianity. We should see with the growth of dispensationalism a development in the level of maturity of the church. We ought to be able to observe that dispensationalists, if their claims are true, should most of all think, act, and speak as the Bible speaks, not just on matters of eschatology, but in all matters of life.

Sadly, dispensationalism has not lent itself to the growth, health, and maturity of the church, but is one of the chief causes of her apparent weakening and stunting, particularly in North America. Wherever dispensationalism is found, one also finds a lack of serious Biblical scholarship and a rather heavy emphasis on the sensational. Strong anti-church sentiments and a severe distrust of any form of faithful ecumenism usually accompany this system. Dispensationalists characteristically espouse an extremely provincial outlook, retreating as far from the world as possible and having little or no multi-generational perspective for either culture or the church.

In order to help us see through to the weaknesses of dispensationalism, we will look at portions of three works from rapture advocate Hal Lindsey who is most recognized for the popular end-times books he has penned over the last three decades.[1] In 1970,

---

1. While some may question whether Lindsey is a credible spokesman for dispensationalism at large, I suggest that he is the best possible spokesman for two reasons. First, his books have been the best selling *non-fiction* end-times books for thirty years. Thus, the ideas in his books have spread to all corners of the church seemingly unabated. Even if more scholarly dispensationalists question his views, the average Christian, it appears, has consumed them with abandon. Second, if more scholarly dispensationalists have questioned his views, they have

he published *The Late Great Planet Earth*, and as a result gained instant notoriety as an end-times expert. By the beginning of 1971, the book was already in its ninth printing and was being consumed by Christians all over the ecclesiastical spectrum. It could be argued that no other book outside of the Bible has had more widespread influence on the church in the last fifty to one hundred years. Eleven years later, Lindsey wrote *The 1980's: Countdown to Armageddon*, following up on some of the themes in the first book and polishing a few other perspectives. Then in 1994, *Planet Earth—2000 A.D.* was published, which was nothing more than a rehash of the 1970 work slightly updated for the coming of the new millennium.

Dispensationalism's Source is Not the Scriptures

We can see through a study of Lindsey's writing that, all of their claims notwithstanding, dispensationalists do not place the Scriptures at the center of their discussion and allow everything else to be defined by what the Bible teaches. Rather, a characteristic of dispensationalist

---

done so behind closed doors. In my research, I have not found a single representative from any of the leading dispensationalist seminaries who has publicly called any of Lindsey's views into question. If they believe that he is in error, then surely someone would have written a rebuttal at some point. In the absence of such a refutation, we can only assume that the leading dispensationalist scholars agree with the bulk of Lindsey's teachings and that he speaks for them.

study is to bring one's own experiences, philosophy, speculation, and the knowledge of what was reported on the evening news to the Scriptures and interpret the Bible in the light of all these external influences. If the Bible does not seem to fit the system, the dispensationalist will give complex, esoteric definitions to simple words in order to shoehorn the Scriptures into their end-times framework.

In *Countdown to Armageddon,* Hal Lindsey does not seem to mind admitting, "Even if I didn't know anything about prophecy, I would know enough from studying what is going on in our world to see that we are headed toward catastrophe,"[2] revealing that the greatest influence upon his theology is not good hermeneutics, but current events. While Lindsey rightly pokes fun at people who pursue astrology as a means of knowing the future,[3] he looks to sources not too much more reliable. A browse through the footnotes of his three books reveals countless references to *Time, U.S. News and World Report, The New York Times,* the *Los Angeles Times, Newsweek,* and scores of other journals, periodicals, and news-reporting services, all which lend

---

2. Hal Lindsey, *The 1980's: Countdown to Armageddon* (Bantam, 1981), 161.

3. Hal Lindsey, *The Late Great Planet Earth* (Grand Rapids, MI: Zondervan, 1971) 12.

supporting evidence to his various claims. While this is not conclusive evidence that the news media are the primary source of Lindsey's theology, it at least allows us to see they are a major contributor.

It is interesting to note how in each of the three decades in which these books appeared, the "signs of the times" changed according to what was happening in the world during that particular period. In *The Late Great Planet Earth*, Lindsey points to early discussion about the European Common Market,[4] the threat of communism,[5] China's successful testing of the hydrogen bomb,[6] and fears of overpopulation and famine.[7] In order to add credibility to his view that the world will end very soon, he quotes a scientist, J. Bruce Griffing, who wrote in 1971, "Unless mankind acts immediately, there will be a worldwide famine in 1985, and the extinction of man within 75 years."[8] We can chortle, recognize the clarity of our hindsight, and give him a break on that one, or we can observe that this is only

---

4. Ibid., 94.

5. Ibid., 95.

6. Ibid., 86.

7. Ibid., 101–2.

8. Ibid., 102.

the beginning of a pattern. Here Lindsey exhibits what becomes a sensationalistic habit of whipping people into a frenzy over any scrap of bad science or speculative fantasy that he can find to support his theology.

At the start of the 1980s, Lindsey wrote *Countdown to Armageddon* and reported that once again, the end was near. How could anyone think otherwise? The late seventies saw an oil crisis,[9] the build-up of the Soviet Union,[10] a renewed interest in UFOs and space,[11] and the appearance of America's newest Middle-Eastern enemy, Iran.[12] The invention of the computer gave Lindsey a world of new ideas about how certain prophecies were going to come to pass.[13] For Lindsey, all of these were certain indicators that "we are the generation the prophets were talking about!"[14]

Thirteen years later, the earth was still spinning on its axis and there were no reports of any nation at-

9. Lindsey, *Countdown to Armageddon*, 54.

10. Ibid., 67.

11. Ibid., 34.

12. Ibid., 81.

13. Ibid., 111.

14. Ibid., back cover.

tempting to forcibly insert computer devices into any-one's foreheads. Yet, feeling the need to update us all on the status of our descent, Lindsey published *Planet Earth—2000 A.D.* Fresh earthquake data, strange weather patterns, deforestation, El Niño, depletion of the ozone layer, proliferation of nuclear weapons, and the AIDS virus were all new proof that the sky was falling.[15]

One could very easily get the impression that Lindsey made a career out of playing to the fears and worries of his audience. Every ten years he must update his work to address new concerns that were not present when he wrote his previous book. Though the march of the Red Army across the globe was a sure sign of the end of the world in the 1970s, he curiously makes no effort to explain how events such as the collapse of communism and the fall of the Soviet Union fit into his previous assertions. Rather, he forges ahead to stir up new angst about the state of the world today.

Dispensationalism must incorporate current events into its framework or else it loses its credibility. Unless there are significant developments on the world scene to prove that we are living in the last days, the entire construct collapses. The result is that the dispensa-

---

15. Hal Lindsey, *Planet Earth—2000 A.D.* (Western Front, Ltd., 1994), 83ff.

tionalist interprets the Bible in terms of current events, rather than interpreting current events using a Biblical framework.

Dispensationalism Mishandles the Scriptures

One simple example of how dispensationalists have traditionally mishandled Scripture to fit the demands of their system is their treatment of the words of Jesus in the Olivet Discourse and in the book of Revelation. In order for dispensationalism to be true, the events that Jesus describes in Matthew 24 and those of the book of Revelation must all be far in the future from the perspective of the New Testament authors. However, a simple reading of the text demands that the events described therein would surely happen within the lifetime of the first century audience.

In Matthew 24:2, Jesus observes the temple and states that "not one stone here will be left upon another, which will not be torn down." His disciples ask him, "When will these things happen, and what will be the sign of Your coming and of the end of the age?" Jesus answers their questions by detailing the events surrounding the beginning of the end and responds to the "when" of their inquiry by stating, "Truly I say to you, this generation will not pass away until all these things take place" (Matt. 24:34). However we choose to understand the events Jesus describes in Matthew 24, we must place them historically within the lifetimes of the people who heard those words, within *that very* generation, or else we do grave injustice to the text.

Likewise, a sense of immediacy is given throughout the book of Revelation. John repeats his message often that the things he describes will happen very soon. The inspired author tells us that these events "must shortly take place" (Rev. 1:1; 22:6), "for the time is near" (1:3; 22:10). Jesus says "I am coming quickly" five times throughout the book (2:16; 3:11; 22:7; 22:12; 22:20). Again, however we choose to interpret the events described in the book of Revelation, we must look for the fulfillment of its prophecies within a few years of its writing. In the closing pages, I will demonstrate how exactly these prophecies were indeed fulfilled within the generation to which Jesus spoke, very shortly after John penned the book of Revelation.

How do dispensationalists handle these texts? In his study Bible, Charles Ryrie comments on Matthew 24:34: "No one living when Jesus spoke these words lived to see 'all these things' come to pass. However, the Greek word can mean 'race' or 'family,' which makes good sense here; i.e., the Jewish race will be preserved, in spite of terrible persecution, until the Lord comes."[16]

One wonders if Ryrie did his own study on this matter, or whether he simply repeated what Scofield said. The comments on this verse in the Ryrie and Scofield Bibles are nearly identical.

The Greek word translated "generation" in Matthew 24:34 is translated "generation" forty-two other times throughout the New Testament, and Ryrie does not take exception to that translation in any other usage. Only when it seems to teach something other than what Ryrie wants it to teach does he seek to redefine the meaning of the word. If what Jesus described in the Olivet Discourse happened before the death of the people standing there that day, dispensationalism crumbles.

On the statement in Revelation 1:1 that these are things "which must soon take place," Ryrie comments: "This word (soon) does not indicate that the events described in this book will necessarily occur soon, but that when they do begin to happen, they will come to pass swiftly."[17]

---

16. Ryrie, 1561.

17. Ryrie, 2013.

For dispensationalists, "generation" does not mean "generation" and "soon" does not mean "soon." Yet they maintain that they alone follow the "plain, normal, literal, historical, and grammatical method of interpretation."[18] We are led to wonder how we can trust the dispensational interpretation of symbolic beasts and numbers when we cannot trust their interpretation of words like "generation" and "soon."

This demonstrates that dispensationalist theology is not driven by a passion to understand what the Scriptures teach, but is clouded by a depression brought on by a pessimistic view of world events. Prophetic passages are read through this filter, and where something does not fit, they redefine simple words so that there are no loose ends to their eschatology. Dispensationalism is anything but a Bible-based theological system.

Dispensationalism Works
Against the Unity of the Church

Within dispensationalism's end-times story is the teaching that the church will not grow into a greater unity and truth, but into greater schism and apostasy. The only churches that will be unified with each other will be liberal, compromised churches. Any concord

---

18. Ryrie, 2076.

among church bodies can only be viewed as a further sign that the end is near. The purest churches, dispensationalism says, will be anti-establishment churches. Their purity will be proven not by their growth, but by their shrinking size and lack of influence.

Lindsey's books are rife with comments such as "when the Rapture occurs, many churches will not have to find a new pastor,"[19] fanning a mistrust for the institution of the church. In *The Late Great Planet Earth* he writes, "The apostate church is, always has been, and will be, the visible, physical gathering of people who may call themselves Christians. These churches may be of any denomination . . . no matter what sacred or holy name is applied to the visible church, this is no guarantee that it teaches and preaches the truth of God. The true church, on the other hand, includes all believers in Christ."[20]

He makes no allowance for Biblical unity among churches, nor does he recognize the authority of the church in any regard. Instead, he works to undermine the unity of the church and teaches Christians to doubt the sincerity and even the salvation of their pastors and fellow church members. Lindsey predicts: "With

---

19. Lindsey, *Planet Earth—2000 A.D.*, 29.

20. Lindsey, *The Late Great Planet Earth*, 127.

increasing frequency the leadership of the denominations will be captured by those who completely reject the historic truths of the Bible . . . [t]he few remaining institutions which are not yet dominated by the disbelievers will go downhill in the same manner. There will be unprecedented mergers of denominations into 'religious conglomerates.' "[21]

Lindsey's rants about a "one-world religion"[22] are not tempered at all with a view to Jesus' desire for his church to be unified. Jesus prayed for his people "that they may all be one; even as you, Father, are in Me and I in You; that they also may be in Us, so that the world may believe that You sent Me" (John 17:21). Neither are Lindsey's predictions about the demise of the church consistent with Jesus' promise that he would build his church and that the "gates of Hades will not overpower it" (Matt. 16:18).

Dispensationalism's view of the church moves in a directly opposite direction from the Bible's. Jesus prayed for a unified church, but dispensationalism fears unity. God's Word teaches that the church will not be overrun by the powers of hell, but dispensation-

21. Lindsey, *The Late Great Planet Earth*, 182.

22. Lindsey, *The Late Great Planet Earth*, 122, 130, 182, 183; Lindsey, *Planet Earth—2000 A.D.*, 43, 201.

alism waits for the destruction and compromise of the Body of Christ.

Dispensationalism Leads to Retreatism

Because of the constant hammering of the one point that this is the last generation before the end, even the most moderate dispensationalist churches have refrained from taking on any work which might not bear immediate fruit. Every mission and ministry of these churches is centered on immediately saving as many individual souls as possible without any vision for the society, culture, or human race at large. As one popular Baptist pastor stated, such broader concerns are simply "polishing the brass on a sinking ship."

Dispensationalists have no multi-generational focus. As they consistently apply their theology to their missions and lives, they find it foolish to take on any effort that may take several years, even several generations to finish. Thus this past century has not been an age of cathedrals, but of pre-fabricated metal buildings.[23] Instead of viewing their own homes and descendents as their greatest mission field and greatest opportunity to

---

23. I recognize that some larger congregations in dispensationalist denominations have begun to build more enduring, traditional places of worship. Perhaps this means that dispensationalism is dying in some circles, or perhaps they still realize that they are going to leave it all to be destroyed when they fly away.

impact the world for the cause of Jesus Christ, they fear bringing children into this cold, cruel world.[24] Rather than seeing to it that their pastors are fully equipped and trained for a long fruitful ministry, the most radical of them ordain men quickly—some of them disdaining seminaries entirely—and get those men into pastorates immediately. They see little need to facilitate the training of great musicians, skilled artists, or gifted writers. There is no time for such efforts. The creation is dying and everything is going down the sewer.

The results of this dogma manifest themselves in the church's steady retreat from society. This has been most notable since Lindsey's first book was published in the 1970s. It has lead Christians to do not much more than wait it out until they are finally evacuated at the rapture. Lindsey expresses this sentiment and asks whether it is time for "Mayflower II":

> There are some Christians and other conservatives who are frankly discussing the possibility of seeking out—like the Mayflower Pilgrims did—another land where people of faith and

---

24. One church I was a member of had several young married couples who decided to take radical surgical procedures against having any children for this very reason. I've known others who have had children, but not without some regret for bringing them into the world.

> freedom can live in peace and liberty . . . Given
> the chill winds of antagonism and ridicule blow-
> ing against Christians in our society, we may in
> our lifetime see the voyage of Mayflower II . . . In
> fact, one organization is actively recruiting free-
> dom-loving citizens (to join) a proposed floating
> city in the Caribbean—complete with parks,
> theaters, schools, shopping, sports facilities and
> ports for aircraft.[25]

The fact is that the first Mayflower was not as
much a retreat from persecution as it was a missionary
effort to create a Christian society on a new continent,
complete with a vision for the evangelization of the na-
tive tribes of North America. The early Puritan settlers
came to America to fulfill the Great Commission, not
just to run from the king.[26] They certainly did not run
to the Americas because they shared Lindsey's view of
the end of the world.

What is most disturbing about Lindsey's writing
here is that he talks about retreating from a culture that
he helped create. When he wrote his first book, the
abortion issue had not yet gone to the Supreme Court,

---

25. *Planet Earth—2000 A.D.,* 276.

26. See Murray.

homosexuality was still taboo, drugs and pornography were nowhere near as prevalent or as accessible as they are today, marriage was still viewed as a sacred union, and outside of a few areas of this country, it was still expected that nearly everyone worshipped in a Christian church on the Lord's Day. Then Lindsey came onto the scene proclaiming that we are living on what will soon be the late great planet Earth. Christians accepted the hype and retreated into their homes and their splintered churches while the world went to hell.

After thirty years of this end-times hysteria, the church has fallen from her former influential position in society. Without any plan for the future, and hardly a plan for the present, the church has lost every single significant cultural battle that has faced our generation. The church keeps thinking that if she can just hold out a little longer, Jesus will come back and everything will be all better. After all, any effort to make this a better world will only delay the second coming.

What they miss in the midst all of this madness is that Jesus placed his church in a position to succeed at her mission. He fully expected her to complete her work and we should not expect him to return until she is finished.[27] The failure of dispensationalists to see

---

27. I'll support these statements in the next section.

that the world is already under the Kingship of Jesus Christ has lead them to accept defeat at the hands of a powerless enemy. Like the Israelite spies who viewed the land of Canaan and shook in fear at the giants they saw there, dispensationalists do not believe their God is mightier than the giants and they do not believe him when he promises to crush the head of the serpent through the means of his triumphant church.

Summary

Darby, Scofield, Ryrie, and Lindsey have taught Christians to look at the world and shake their heads—to concede that any effort to change things is futile. They have turned them away from the Bible and toward the newspaper. They have worked against the God-ordained unity of his church. They have stolen the joy of the church in bearing the fruit of multi-generational work. They have stricken fear into the hearts of God's people and have arrested the advance of the Gospel.

Dispensationalism and its belief in an imminent second coming have failed the church. For nearly two hundred years it has been telling her that the end is near, weakening her walls and making her impotent against her enemies. One wonders how much longer this teaching will be tolerated. As successive generations hear the railing of end times prophets, and continue to see the failure of their false prophecies, the church will return to the historical doctrine of a victorious church—a triumphant gospel—and get back to work.

An Alternate Perspective

There is another, more consistent way of interpreting the Scriptures that does not demand an "any-minute" return of Christ, and it is a view that has certainly been around a lot longer. In the days when it was the most widely-held position, it produced an unparalleled level of kingdom activity, missionary endeavor, and church health. This is the view which asserts that Jesus began his reign as King during his first earthly ministry.

When Christ came to earth over two thousand years ago, he came to inaugurate his kingdom *successfully*. During his ministry here, he bound Satan. Within a generation of his crucifixion he destroyed the old world of the old covenant and ushered in a new heavens and a new earth. The church is now the Holy City of God and all of the nations are brought into it. She will continue to preach the gospel on earth for thousands upon thousands of years, progressively growing in number and strength until one day, far in the future, the entire world will be transformed by the power of Christ and an Eden-like paradise will be restored. At some point in that golden day, Christ will return to judge the living and the dead. Those who rejected the gospel will be sent to eternal punishment. The dead in Christ will be raised, joined to their resurrected bodies, and all of the saints of all of the ages will live together in union and communion with the Triune God for eternity.

Perhaps these words sound a little heretical and possibly downright blasphemous to someone who has never known anything other than dispensational eschatology. Rest assured that each of these points depends on nothing more than a simple reading of Scripture and a short history lesson on the events of 70 A.D. Be also mindful that the majority of Bible scholars throughout the history of the church read the Scriptures in somewhat the same manner as this.

What the Psalms Say About the Kingdom of Christ

In order to understand how the Old Testament saints thought and spoke about God's plan for the future, we may begin by viewing the manner in which the Psalms speak of the coming Messiah and the nature of his kingdom. New Testament writers quote or refer to Psalm 110 more than any other Old Testament passage.[1] This psalm builds the theology of the King and his kingdom that was foundational to the New Covenant message. In order for first-century Jews to rightly understand Messiah, they had to rightly understand the message of Psalm 110:

> The Lord said unto my Lord, Sit thou at my right hand, until I make thine enemies thy footstool. The Lord shall send the rod of thy strength out of Zion: rule thou in the midst of thine enemies. Thy people shall be willing in the day of thy power, in the beauty of holiness from the womb of the morning: thou hast the dew of thy youth. The Lord hath sworn, and will not repent, Thou art a priest for ever after the order of Melchizedek. The Lord at thy right hand shall strike through kings in the day of his wrath. He shall judge among the heathen, he shall fill the places with the dead bodies; he shall wound the heads over many countries. He shall drink of the brook in the way: therefore shall he lift up the head.

---

1. . Matt. 22:41–45; Mark 12:35–37; Luke 20:41–44; Acts 2:33–35; 1 Cor. 15:25; Heb. 1:13; 5:6; 7:17, 21; 10:13.

This psalm pronounces God's objective that the rule of Messiah be a reign that would take place at the Father's own right hand. It teaches that Jesus is ruling right now from his throne in heaven. For the psalmist David, it was not necessary for Christ to be present physically on the earth to wage war against his enemies. We see here in this psalm the details of a battle in progress with a sure outcome of victory for the King. His enemies will certainly be made a footstool under his rule, and until they are vanquished he will not leave the Father's right hand.

While apparently many of the Jews of Jesus' day missed the point of this psalm, expecting the Messiah to gain an immediate military and political victory over his enemies, the apostle Paul reminded them that "now is Christ risen from the dead, and become the firstfruits of them that slept" (1 Cor. 15:20), and then, quoting Psalm 110, "For he must reign till he hath put all enemies under his feet." (1 Cor. 15:25). Christ did not fail in his mission, for his mission was not to set up a palace in downtown Jerusalem. Paul comforts the church with the message that the risen and ascended Christ is now in a superior position from which to carry out his program of putting "all things under his feet" (1 Cor. 15:27), and that his reign does not only *begin* with the defeat of his enemies, but lasts all the way through the act of their suppression. He remains seated on his throne next to his Father and does not come back to earth until his enemies are overthrown.

Another psalm important to our study is Psalm 22, which details the suffering of the Christ which was yet to come. After a mournful description of the Savior's passion, the psalmist breaks out in a song of victory: "All the ends of the world shall remember and turn unto the Lord: and all the kindreds of the nations shall worship before thee. For the kingdom is the Lord's and he is the governor among the nations" (Ps. 22:27–28).

If any psalm should be sung in the minor key, it is Psalm 22. Beginning with the woeful "My God, my God, why hast thou forsaken me? Why art thou so far from helping me and from the words of my roaring?" the subject matter through the first three-quarters of the psalm overflows with gravity and sobriety. If it were true that the sacrifice of Christ would only reap the most meager of a harvest of souls, the crucifixion would preface a couple of thousand years of increasing apostasy and declining morality, and the occasion of the passion of Christ was to be only a tiny part of the greater tragedy of the total failure of God's plan for the salvation of the world, then the psalmist would not even have to change keys to tell the rest of the story in song. He could have kept right on with the sad events and proclaimed the further sinfulness and final collapse of the people of God.

But he doesn't. At the end of Psalm 22, David declares the victory of the gospel to the ends of the world. It is not just a vague hope, but an inspired confidence that leads him to write that all of the world should turn to the Lord and that all of the nations should worship him. Just as surely as the first section of the psalm was fulfilled in the crucifixion of Christ, so also will the last section be fulfilled when all the people of the world acknowledge him as King.

One more key insight into the view of the future presented in the psalms is found in Psalm 105:7–8: "He is the Lord our God: his judgments are in all the earth. He hath remembered his covenant for ever, the word which he commanded to a thousand generations." From the perspective of this psalm there is still a lot of future to be lived in the light of the covenant promises of God. The psalmist expects there to be *at least* one thousand generations to reap the benefits of the covenant of the Lord. Usually when the Scriptures use big round numbers like "a thousand," it is taken to mean an innumerable amount far beyond one thousand. For example, Psalm 50:10 tells us that God owns the cattle upon a thousand hills. This does not mean that someone else owns the cattle on the one-thousand-and-first hill. It is a figurative means of saying that God owns the cattle on an innumerable amount of hills. In other words, God owns all the cows.

Psalm 105 could be indicating that God has directed his word to thousands upon thousands of generations, in which case we are not even close to seeing the last generation. But for argument's sake, if Jesus plans to return again to judge the earth after the one-thousandth generation, we are still very, very far from that point in time. If a new generation is born every twenty years, then we are roughly one hundred generations removed from Christ's generation, and at most only about three hundred generations removed from Adam. Using the most conservative estimate, the one-thousandth generation of mankind will not be born until 16,000 A.D. Certainly the point of this passage is not for us to draw a timeline, but to let us know that God intends to be gracious to thousands of generations.

To pull the messages of these three psalms together, first we read that Jesus does not have to leave his throne in heaven in order to reign as King. In fact, he will not leave that position until his enemies have been defeated. Second, the growth of his kingdom will continue until all the people of the world turn and worship the Lord. Third, from the perspective of the psalmist, there is yet an immense amount of time ahead in order for God's purposes to be worked out.

Already, there is a great deal of disagreement between what the Scriptures teach about the future and what dispensationalism says. In dispensationalism, Christ leaves heaven to fight an epic military battle to win his victory and defeat his enemies. According to dispensationalism, the story of the church is one of increasing weakness and failure until Jesus finally comes back to rapture a very small handful of the faithful. Dispensationalists tell us that there is precious little time left and that the end of the world could come any day. These teachings oppose the Scriptures. The Bible simply does not talk the way dispensationalism talks.

What the Prophets Say About the Kingdom of Christ

The prophets concur with the psalms on the matter of Christ's kingdom. They saw no intervening period between the time of his first coming and his rule as King over all the earth. They speak only of the progressive increase of his rule and of his victory over his enemies. Isaiah wrote of the coming Messiah:

> For unto us a child is born, unto us a son is given:
> and the government shall be upon his shoulder;

and his name shall be called Wonderful, Coun-
sellor, The mighty God, The everlasting Father,
The Prince of Peace. Of the increase of his government and peace there shall be no end, upon
the throne of David and upon his kingdom, to
order it, and to establish it with judgment and
with justice from henceforth even for ever. The
zeal of the Lord of hosts will perform this. (Isaiah 9:6–7)

In this particular passage, there is no extended period of time mentioned between the event of the birth
of Messiah and the establishment of his kingdom, but
rather his coming *is* the establishment of his kingdom.
His is a kingdom on the advance from its inception,
increasing in influence through the ages, without end.
Isaiah assures us that it is no less than the zeal of the
Lord of hosts which is the motivation for this un-
dertaking. He will zealously accomplish this mission
without abatement or delay. He is not speaking of an
enterprise that can be thwarted or delayed by the unbelief of either Jew or Gentile. What is in view is the
entire scope of the purposes of the coming Messiah.

Isaiah writes much about the glorious golden age
that the reign of Messiah will bring about, telling us
that one day "the earth shall be full of the knowledge

of the Lord, as the waters cover the sea" (Isaiah 11:9), and he concludes the last chapter of his book with the words:

> For I know their works and their thoughts: it shall come, that I will gather all nations and tongues; and they shall come, and see my glory. For as the new heavens and the new earth, which I will make, shall remain before me, saith the Lord, so shall your seed and your name remain. And it shall come to pass, that from one new moon to another, shall all flesh come to worship before me, saith the Lord. (Is. 66:18, 22–23)

Zechariah preached the same message:

> Rejoice greatly, O daughter of Zion: shout, O daughter of Jerusalem: behold thy King cometh unto thee: he is just, and having salvation: lowly and riding upon an ass, and upon a colt the foal of an ass. And I will cut off the chariot from Ephraim, and the horse from Jerusalem, and the battle bow shall be cut off: and he shall speak peace unto the heathen: and his dominion shall be from sea even to sea, and from the river even to the ends of the earth. (Zech. 9:9–10)

Jeremiah concurred:

> But this shall be the covenant that I will make
> with the house of Israel; after those days, saith
> the Lord, I will put my law in their inward parts
> and write it in their hearts; and will be their
> God and they shall be my people. And they shall
> teach no more every man his neighbour, and ev-
> ery man his brother, saying, Know the Lord; for
> they shall all know me, from the least of them
> unto the greatest of them, saith the Lord, for I
> will forgive their iniquity, and I will remember
> their sin no more. (Jer. 31:33–34)

The common theme we see throughout the Old
Testament prophets is the expectation that the first
coming of Messiah would be the beginning of not just a
new dispensation of grace, but the beginning of a gold-
en age. Such was their vision of this glorious age that it
was not an exaggeration for them to refer to it as a "new
heaven and new earth." With the coming of Messiah,
the old world with its old covenant and old system was
to pass away. All things were to become new with Jesus.

The concept that the golden age could only become a reality within a magical one-thousand-year
political reign of Jesus upon his second coming was a
foreign idea to the prophets. In the Zechariah passage

above, the prophet does not put any separation between Jesus' entrance into Jerusalem on a donkey and his taking up the task of putting the whole earth under his dominion. Jeremiah saw the introduction of the New Covenant as concomitant with the beginning of global evangelization. One flows out of the other and they cannot be separated.

It cannot be stressed too much that the prophets did not teach that the golden age of the gospel was contingent upon a second coming of Christ a couple thousand years after the resurrection. Nor did they teach that it was only a hopeful possibility that would most likely be superseded by the failure of the people of God to complete their task, thus requiring Christ to come rapture them and bail them out of the program. According to the prophets, the work of saving the world began with Christ's first coming, and that work is most certainly going to be successful. If we are to believe the prophets, we would look forward to a time in the future when the entire world will worship the Triune God through Jesus Christ as a result of the advancement of the kingdom he began in his earthly ministry.

Dispensationalism insists that Christ must first return to earth before the world will worship him. The reasoning goes that the prophets did not see a gap between Christ's first coming and the evangelization of the world because they could not account for Israel's unbelief. Because Israel rejected Messiah, dispensationalists say, God established the church and put his plan on hold until Israel could get itself back together. It is suggested that he will give it another try after he raptures his church and comes back to enforce his plan as a political king in Jerusalem. Then and only then will the earth be full of the knowledge of the Lord.

These thoughts are alien to the natural reading of the prophets. Jeremiah, Zechariah, and Isaiah saw a seamless coming of Messiah and an unfolding of his progressive work to bring all the nations under his rule. If God chose not to reveal to them such a major portion of his plan, as it seems that dispensationalists are suggesting, then it is hard to see how the writings of the prophets would be useful to the church at all, blind and deluded as the prophets would have been to the reality of this other plan that God had waiting in the wings. On the contrary, the words of the prophets are of vital importance to the church, because God revealed the entire scope of his agenda to them.

What Did Jesus Say About His Kingdom?

If the disbelief of the Jews was an unforeseeable circumstance to Jesus and if he considered putting his kingdom on the back burner until some other things could be sorted out, it is hardly conceivable that he would have pronounced the coming of his kingdom so emphatically. In Matthew's gospel alone, Jesus proclaims the arrival of the kingdom no less than fifty times. When he repeatedly declares that "the Kingdom is at hand," he is pronouncing his fulfillment of the promises made to the prophets that Messiah would come to establish his kingdom and that his kingdom would have no end. As David Chilton points out, Jesus did not talk about his kingdom as if it were something that would exist far into the future.

> Jesus clearly told Israel to repent *now*, because the Kingdom was coming *soon*. The Kingdom was *at hand*. He was bringing it in right before their eyes, and soon would ascend to the Father to sit on the throne of the Kingdom. This is why He told His disciples, "Assuredly, I say to you, there are some standing here who will not taste death until they see the Son of Man coming in His Kingdom" (Matthew 16:28). Was Jesus right or wrong? In terms of some modern teachers, Jesus was mistaken. And this was no slight miscalculation: Jesus missed the mark by thousands of years! Can we trust Him as Lord and Savior, and still hold that he was wrong, or that somehow His prophecy got derailed? We

must believe what Jesus said: within the lifetime of those who were listening to Him, He would come in His Kingdom. And that is exactly what he did, culminating in His ascension to His heavenly throne.[2]

In his "Kingdom Parables," Jesus taught that from its beginning the kingdom would continue to develop progressively and grow stronger until all of the nations were under its care and benefit from its splendor. These parables repeat the message throughout the gospels that the kingdom starts small, but grows in might and glory. The parable of the mustard seed is just one example. "He presented another parable to them, saying, 'The kingdom of heaven is like a mustard seed, which a man took and sowed in his field; and this is smaller than all the other seeds, but when it is full grown, it is larger than the garden plants and becomes a tree, so that the birds of the air come and nest in its branches'" (Matt. 13:31–32).

This parable is the story of the church. It began small like a mustard seed, with only a handful of men in an insignificant dot on a map. In the ages since, it

---

2. . David Chilton, *Paradise Restored* (Ft. Worth, TX: Dominion Press, 1981), 70.

has grown to all corners of the world, shaping culture, turning men to Christ, and making the world a better place to live. It will continue to grow until all the world is converted.

Jesus asked the Father in his model prayer that "Thy kingdom come, Thy will be done on Earth as it is heaven" (Matt. 6:10). If we can assume that God answers his Son's prayers, the request that God's will be done on Earth as it is in heaven is seen in the progressive shaping of the cultures of men to conform to the culture of heaven. This is the work that Jesus commissioned the church to do when he commanded them to make disciples of all the nations. In promising her that he would be with her throughout all ages, he affirmed that he would not allow his church to fail in the task to which he has assigned her.

The message that the church will grow weaker and weaker throughout the years until it fades out in a tiny ember is entirely inconsistent with the message of the kingdom that Jesus preached. Jesus was optimistic about the prospects of his people under his reign. He did not set them up for failure, but for victory.

Back When the World Ended

If we are not, then, to think about a future full of fire and brimstone, but rather full of victory for the church, then what are we to make of those sections of Scripture that dispensationalists continually use to talk about the destruction of the world and the rapture of the church? As stated in another section, when Jesus spoke about the "end of the world" and the "end of the age," he was clear to state that these events would happen within a generation of the time that he spoke those words. So, too, the book of Revelation repeatedly makes reference that the things about which it speaks will shortly come to pass.

The events that Jesus describes in Matthew 24 and those events described in the book of Revelation did indeed happen in the time frame that the Scriptures provide. In the year 70 AD there was untold suffering by the people of Jerusalem as the Roman armies surrounded the city and destroyed the temple. The historian Josephus describes in graphic detail the awful ways in which the Romans treated the Jews and the terrible things the Jews did to each other. It was a time of chaos and misery, and it was the way that God pronounced his final judgment on Israel and brought an end to the old world.

With the fall of the temple, the final nail had been driven in the old covenant world's coffin. The days of great tribulation leading up to the fall of Jerusalem were, in fact, the last days of Israel. It is not uncommon in the Scriptures to see such apocalyptic language used when God judges a nation. As James Jordan demonstrates, God used similar "last days" language in Isaiah 13 when he sought to judge Babylon:

> Isaiah 13:9–10 says that "the day of the Lord is coming," and when it comes, "the stars of heaven and their constellations will not flash forth their light; the sun will be dark when it rises, and the moon will not shed its light." It goes on to say in verse 13, "I shall make the heavens tremble,

and the earth will be shaken from its place at the fury of the Lord of hosts in the day of His burning anger."

Well, this certainly does sound like the end of the world! But if we read these verses in context, we have to change our initial impression. Verse 1 says, "The oracle concerning Babylon which Isaiah the son of Amoz saw," and if we read on, we find nothing to indicate any change in subject. It is the end of Babylon—not the end of the world—that is spoken of. In fact, in verse 17, God says that he will "stir up the Medes against them," so that the entire chapter is clearly concerned only with Babylon's destruction. If we read Biblically, this won't seem so strange. What verse 10 is saying is that Babylon's lights are going to go out. Their clocks are going to stop. Their day is over, and it is the day of doom for them.[1]

If the reader will put all of the passages about the end of the world in the context of the destruction of Jerusalem, he will find that there need not be any fanciful speculation about certain events or characters, but that everything therein fits neatly into what has al-

---

1. . James Jordan, *Through New Eyes* (Eugene, OR: Wipf and Stock, 1999), 62.

ready happened two thousand years ago.[2] The last days of Jerusalem have come and are over. God ended that world, and in Christ he ushered in a new world—our world. He has bound Satan, and we are now reigning with Christ as his brethren and co-heirs, working to bring the nations under his rule.

We can then read the passages about resurrection and our future with Christ with a clearer head. Jesus will return a second time, but it will only be after the church has completed her assignment and his enemies have been made his footstool. As much as we might like to be the special generation that gets to see this happen, this is not going to happen in our lifetime. There is too much work left to be done.

The Fruit of This View

The view presented here is a historic, orthodox view, long held by the church. Wherever this manner of

---

2. . Even 2 Peter 3, which has been used to argue against the position I am advocating, is more easily understood if placed within the context of the events of the first century. Peter wrote this before Jerusalem fell and is telling those people living in that very day that the world they know is about to be destroyed, and he is giving them direction on how to live during that time. He tells them that the promise of the coming of the judgment of the Lord is about to be fulfilled and that they should be vigilant. If this does not have a first century application, then Peter is actively deceiving every single generation except the last in promising them something that will not happen in their lifetime.

reading the Scriptures and understanding the kingdom is applied, the church has grown strong, missionary zeal has bloomed, and countless souls have turned to Christ.

In *The Puritan Hope*, Iain Murray includes a description of seventeenth-century Scotland where these thoughts were most prevalent:

> Every parish had a minister, every village had a school, every family almost had a Bible . . . Every minister was obliged to preach thrice a week, to lecture and catechise once, besides other private duties wherein they abounded, according to their proportion of faithfulness and abilities. None of them might be scandalous in their conversation, or negligent in their office . . . Indeed, in many places the spirit seemed to be poured out with the Word . . . (indicated) by the multitude of sincere converts. I have lived many years in a parish where I never heard an oath, and you might have ridden many miles before you heard any: Also, you could not for a great part of the country have lodged in a family where the Lord was not worshipped by reading, singing and publick prayer. No body complained more of our church government than our taverners,

whose ordinary lamentation was, their trade was
broke, people were become so sober.[3]

This theology has fueled the most ambitious missionary endeavors the church has ever seen. Believing
in a victorious church, missionary William Carey left
for India, David Livingstone headed to Africa, and
David Brainerd went to the American Indians. They
began their missions with the idea that they were start-
ing works which would have results reaching far into
the future. Murray comments, "They did not regard
the number of individual converts in the present as
the first consideration, but rather that energy should
be deployed in work which would have the maximum
influence upon nations in subsequent generations."[4]
Only with an understanding that the kingdom will one
day cover the earth can the church consistently take on
any task that will have any lasting value. Dispensationalism may create a stir and some excitement, but it is
not built for the long haul. Any effort driven by dispensational adrenaline is ultimately sloppy and short-lived.
It is engineered for obsolescence.

---

3. . Murray, *The Puritan Hope*, 34–35.

4. . Ibid., 180.

My hope for the one who is anxious about the end of the world is that he will reconsider his position, realizing its faulty foundations. We must realize that we no longer need to live life in fear that the end of the world could come at any moment. We can confidently make plans for our children and grandchildren and great-grandchildren. We can work with great hope that our labor is not in vain, but that our work will have long-lasting results, reaching far into the future. We can know that even now Christ is reigning at the right hand of the Father and is progressively crushing the head of the enemy.

We can also breathe easy, remembering that all the doomsayers and all the apocalyptic date-setters have always been wrong. The Hal Lindseys and the radical environmentalists together have to keep resetting their clocks and find new indicators that the end is near, lest they lose their audience and, most importantly, their funding.

Taking this fresh perspective, new light shines on the Apostle Paul's words in Romans 8:28, that "all things work together for good to those who love God, to those who are the called according to His purpose." We can take up a sure hope that all of creation is under the sovereign direction of Christ the King and it is all working together for the good of his people, yesterday, today, and tomorrow. This means not only will they go to be with the Lord when they die, but that presently, in the world, God's kingdom is advancing for the glory of his name and the good of his people.

We can take Christ at his word that his kingdom is in place. We can re-engage the culture, knowing that the victory is ours. This world is ours for the taking. Christ has promised that we will not be vanquished, but will reign with him. The zeal of the Lord of Hosts will perform this.